BATGIRL

Fists of Fury

Batgirl: Fists of Fury

DC Comics, 1700 Broadway, New York, NY 10019
A Warner Bros. Entertainment Company
Printed in Canada. First Printing.
ISBN: 1-4012-0203-5
Cover art by Damion Scott & Robert Campanella
Cover color by Tom McCraw

Fists of Fury

Kelley Puckett
Scott Peterson
Writers

Damion Scott
Vincent Giarrano
Phil Noto
Pencillers

Robert Campanella
Jesse Delperdang
Inkers

Jason Wright
Gregory Wright
Colorists

John Costanza
Letterer

Damion Scott, Robert Campanella
& John Lowe
Tim Sale
Original Covers

Batman created by Bob Kane

WHO'S THAT GIRL...?

Cassandra Cain isn't a typical teenager. Her father is David Cain, an assassin whose skills are so formidable, he was once called upon to train Batman himself. David Cain passed on his voluminous knowledge of the art of combat to his only daughter. Every ounce of her energy was devoted to learning his brutal skills...even at the expense of her speech. Though trained to be the perfect assassin, Cassandra eventually decided that her father's ways were not her own. She left him and was found on the streets of Gotham by the original Batgirl, Barbara Gordon. With the blessing of Barbara, Cassandra was asked to join Batman's crusade as the new Batgirl. In the months following No Man's Land, she continued the quest for justice under Barbara's mentorship. Cassandra learned to speak with the help of a telepath, but her new verbal skills impeded her ability to read body language and thus predict her opponent's moves. The martial artist and assassin Lady Shiva helped her regain that talent, and now Batgirl is considered one of the greatest martial artists in the world.

She looked
into his eyes,
eyes she would
never really
know, and said
HM.
...EYES... NEVER REALLY KNOW...
...AND SAID...

BAM

UNBELIEVABLE! IT'S GETTING LOUDER!

WHAT THE HELL IS GOING--

MAY GOD HAVE MERCY ON YOUR SOUL.

TAP TAP
OPEN UP, CHILDREN. GOD'S JUSTICE IS MERCIFUL AND SWIFT.
SOUL STICE
WHAM
TIK

AASH
THOK
TUNK

RAX
PLEASE, I... PLEASE TELL ME WHAT I'M DOING HERE...
INSANE.

AAAAAAHH!!
BUDDA
BUDDA
BUDDA
BUDDA

AAAAHH!!
BUDDA
BUDDA
BUDDA
BUDDA

HURGH

DAMMIT, I'M OUT!
I NEED AMMO!

GRENADE!
THAP
KCHNK
PLAF

WHOK
WHOK
BOOOOM

TWO LUNATICS.
SEVEN BLOCKS.
HM.

NO!
NO, PLEASE!

GIVE ME YOUR HAND.
BATMAN?
YOU WERE KNOCKED UNCONSCIOUS. TAKE IT SLOWLY.

THERE... THERE WERE...
TWO LUNATICS, I KNOW. THEY WERE NORMAL CITIZENS, DRIVEN INSANE...
...BY THE JOKER.

JOKER? I DON'T... THERE WAS... A MACHINE...
BATGIRL. YOU'RE CONFUSED. YOU HAVE A HEAD INJURY.

DO YOU TRUST ME?
OF COURSE.

THEN LET'S GO.

JOLLY KIDS CIRCUS
CLOSED
JOKER'S INSIDE. HIS MEN AREN'T.
GUARD THE ENTRANCE. I'LL TAKE CARE OF THE REST.
YOU OKAY?
FINE.
THANKS.
BLAM

BATMAN?
OOPS!
I...DID IT AGAIN.
I splattered your heaaart, all over the ground, ooh, now baby--
--I JUST CANNOT GET THAT CATCHY LITTLE THING OUT OF MY HEAD!

BATMAN!
DEAD, IS HE?
HM. YES.

WELL, NOW... WHAT AM I GOING TO DO WITH ALL THIS FREE TIME? I GUESS I COULD TAKE UP NEEDLEPOINT...

...OR RUNNING.

I'M SORRY.
Ooh, now baby, baby...
OOPS! I--

KRAK

WHAM
WHAT'S THIS? ABUSING THE HANDICAPPED? SOCIETY FROWNS ON THAT, YOU KNOW.
WHAT WOULD BATMAN THINK?
HE'S DEAD.
AND SO ARE YOU.

WHBAAAM

TINK
TAK
TOK
SZZT
EXPLAIN.
UM, WELL...
...MY INVENTION EMPLOYS A FORM OF LOW FREQUENCY MODULATION TO DIRECTLY PROPAGATE A PARTICULAR WAVEFORM ALONG THE SURFACE OF THE LOWER PREFRONTAL--
ENGLISH.
NGK! IT'S... IT MAKES YOU KILL. MAKES YOU... DECIDE TO KILL.
AND HAVING DECIDED TO KILL, THE BRAIN THEN FORMS ITS OWN SCENARIOS TO JUSTIFY THE KILLING, YOU SEE?
THE PRIEST'S BRAIN USED RELIGION AS AN EXCUSE. THE VETERAN'S USED WAR.

THEN... WHY ME?
YES, THAT...WASN'T SUCH A GOOD IDEA, WAS IT. I ASSURE YOU I DIDN'T WANT TO DIE, IT'S JUST THAT I...I DIDN'T ANTICIPATE YOUR REACTION.
YOU SEE, I'D MEANT TO STUN YOU--THE BEAM PUTS ONE IN A CATATONIC STATE WHILE THE BRAIN CONSTRUCTS ITS FANTASY SCENARIO.

THE VET WAS IN THAT STATE FOR TEN MINUTES BEFORE HE STARTED KILLING. FOR THE PRIEST, IT WAS AN HOUR.
BUT FOR YOU...
...IT WAS A HEARTBEAT.

I CAME TO SAY I'LL BE OUT OF TOWN FOR A FEW HOURS, MAYBE MORE. PRISON RIOT.
WHAT HAPPENED HERE?
NOT SURE.
BATMAN?
YES?
BE CAREFUL.
Writer
KELLEY PUCKETT
Penciller
DAMION SCOTT
Inker
ROBERT CAMPANELLA
Colorist
JASON WRIGHT
Separator
DIGITAL CHAMELEON
Letterer
JOHN COSTANZA
Editor
MICHAEL WRIGHT

SPLAT

OUTSIDE! THAT'S A MISS!
GROSS!
EW!
WAIT--ONLY HALF OF IT'S OUT!
NO WAY, DOESN'T COUNT.
I GET THIS ONE, I WIN.

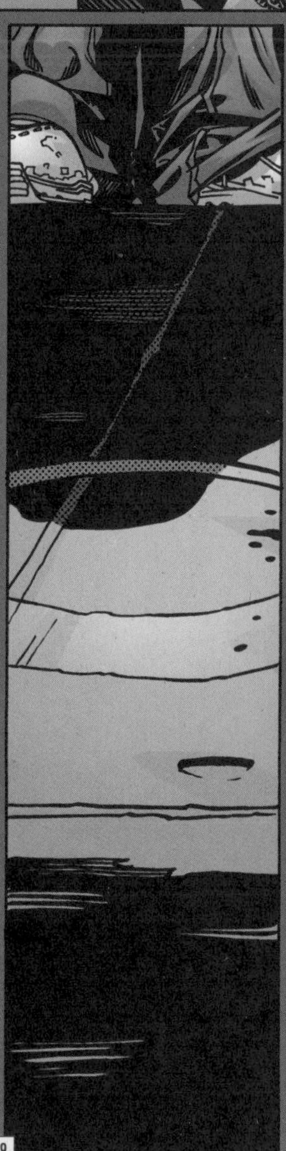

AAAAA!
RUUN!

UH...
I'M SORRY.
GOOD.
COULD YOU...
...COULD YOU COME WITH ME? I HAVE TO SHOW YOU SOMETHING.
UH... NO. I...
IT'S, UH... IT'S JUST THAT...
...I THINK MY DAD MIGHT BE DOING SOMETHING BAD.

MY NAME'S TIM, COME ON IN.
I HEARD DAD ON THE PHONE, TALKING TO HIS FRIENDS...
DO NOT REMOVE
HE DIDN'T KNOW I WAS LISTENING AND THEY TALKED ABOUT ROBBING SOMEPLACE.
THEN HE LEFT AND TOLD ME NOT TO STAY UP AND...
...AND HE TOOK HIS GUNS.
THIS IS WHERE THEY WENT.

READ IT.
YOU CAN'T READ?
IT SAYS "GOTHAM FEDERAL BANK, 420 ROBINSON STREET."
AIT...
MY DAD'S NOT A BAD MAN.
HE JUST THINKS ABOUT MONEY TOO MUCH.
PLEASE STOP HIM... BEFORE HE DOES SOMETHING BAD.

...FLYIN' STRAIGHT TO RIO, BABY.
HELL, YEAH. I'M A GET ME ONE A THOSE GIRLS FROM IPANEMA, JUST LAY OUT ON THE BEACH AND WATCH THE TIDE ROLL IN.
GOTHAM FEDERAL BANK
WATCHU DOIN' WIT' YOUR TAKE, JAKE?
PAY SOME BILLS.
BETTER BE A CLOTHING BILL, BABY, CUZ YOU LOOK BAD. I MEAN... I'M ASHAMED TO ROB BANKS WITH YOU.

AND GET YOURSELF A REAL GUN. WHAT IS THAT, YOUR DADDY'S VIETNAM GUN OR SOMETHING?
DAMN. JAKE. I BET THAT THING DON'T EVEN--
HANDS IN THE--
BLAM!
HNK
WHUMP

DAMN, JAKE.
WHAT THE HELL'S GOING--
OH.
HUH. MUST'VE BEEN HIDING.
NICE JOB, JAKE.
DIDN'T THINK YOU HAD IT IN YOU.
LET'S GO, LADIES. TIME TO GET WHAT WE CAME FOR.

WELL, ALL RIGHT. SEVEN OF US. SEVEN CARTS OF CASH.
MOVE 'EM OUT.

KINDA HEAVY, HUH.
HELL, YEAH.
HEY, TONY.
YEAH?

WHAT'S THAT?
WHAT'S WHAT?

BLAM!

DAMN, CHACO!
WHAT THE HELL...?
EVERYBODY SEE THAT? ALL TRACEABLE.
DAMN FOOL HAD HIS OWN CART OF CASH...STILL HAD TO TAKE MORE.
YOU GET GREEDY... AND EVERYTHING GOES TO HELL.
KNOW THAT.
HEY...
...WHERE THE HELL IS JAKE?

DEAD END.

YOU... YOU DON'T WANT TO DO THIS.
YOU SHOULDN'A RUN, JAKE.
YEAH, MAN. NOT SMART.
YOU THREATENING ME, JAKE?
I'M PROMISING YOU.
YOU DON'T WANT TO FEEL WHAT I'M FEELING.
I AIN'T LIKE YOU, JAKE. AND THAT'S A LOT OF MONEY WAITIN' FOR ME BACK THERE.
SORRY, MAN.

CHOK
THAM

GO.
NO. I... KILLED A MAN.
I... NEED TO PAY.

ALL RIGHT.
WHAT ABOUT...
...YOUR SON?
MY SON?
I DON'T HAVE A SON.
WHAT? BUT...
...TIM.
TIM? I DON'T... OH.
YOU'RE THINKING OF CHACO'S KID.

...THE HELL IS TAKING THEM SO LONG...
THAT'S IT. LET'S GO. COME ON. MOVE.
WHAT?
WE CAN'T JUST LEAVE THEM.
YOU CAN SPLIT THEIR TAKE. YOU READY NOW?
YEAH, ALL RIGHT.
I'M COOL.
YEAH, THOUGHT SO.

WHAM

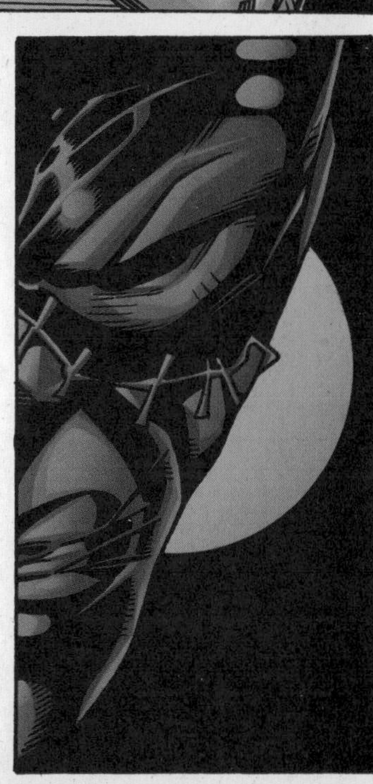

CHOK!
WHOK!
THAK!

GCPD
DAD?
HT
NITE
LAN
TIM.
LET'S...
GO HOME.
OKAY.

MY DAD...
...HE'S BAD. ISN'T HE?
YES. HE IS.
BUT... YOU'RE... NOT.
OKAY?
Writer KELLEY PUCKETT
Penciller DAMION SCOTT
Inker ROBERT CAMPANELLA
Colorist JASON WRIGHT
Separator DIGITAL CHAMELEON
Letterer JOHN COSTANZA
Editor MICHAEL WRIGHT

KRK
KRKK
KKKK

UH...
FRIEND?
BLUUAH
EW!

UW... WOO...
WHAT'S THAT? YOU OKAY?
WW... WH. WH.
WHY...

...AM I HERE? ORACLE SENT ME TO GET YOU.
SHE'S BEEN CALLING YOU FOR TEN HOURS. WHAT'VE YOU BEEN DOING...
...ALL THIS TIME?
LET'S GO.
WAIT... ORACLE SAID TO--

--TOOK THE TUNNELS LIKE I SAID?
GOOD. HAVE A SEAT, SPOILER.
WHAT'S THIS?
BATGIRL. YOU HAVEN'T BEEN STUDYING YOUR SUPER-VILLAIN FILES BY ANY CHANCE, HAVE YOU?
WHAT? NO. NO. WHY--?
RELAX-- I DIDN'T THINK YOU HAD.
LONG STORY SHORT--THE JOKER BROKE OUT ABOUT A HUNDRED CRIMINALS, TURNED THEM INSANE JUST LIKE HIM, AND SENT THEM ON A RAMPAGE.
AND ALMOST ALL OF THEM ARE SUPERHUMAN.

NOW, LISTEN-- I KNOW YOU THINK YOU CAN BEAT ANYONE AND I KNOW YOU THINK YOU'RE RESPONSIBLE FOR EVERYONE IN GOTHAM, BUT YOU'RE NOT.
YOU DON'T KNOW WHAT THESE VILLAINS' POWERS ARE AND YOU'RE NOT PREPARED TO FIGHT THEM. I WANT YOU TO STAY RIGHT HERE WITH ME UNTIL THIS IS OVER.
OKAY?
WELL... GOOD. OKAY, THEN.
HOLO-ROOM OPEN?
OKAY.
YEAH. SURE. GO AHEAD.
HEY, ARE YOU GOING TO TRAIN?
WHAT?
IS IT OKAY IF I WATCH? I COULD REALLY LEARN--
NO.

SNIK
LOCK DOOR.
GOTHAM CITY.
NIGHT.
DEATHMATCH.
COMBAT CONFIGURATION?
BATGIRL.
EXECUTING CUSTOM CONFIGURATION BATGIRL:
SPEED: MAXIMUM
COMBAT LEVEL: MAXIMUM
SAFETIES OFF
OPPONENT?

BO-RING...
THESE ENERGY READINGS DON'T MAKE SENSE...
HEY, DID YOU PAY YOUR ELECTRIC BILL? THE LIGHTS ARE BLINKING.
I BROKE IT.
SORRY.
YOU BROKE... THE ROOM?
ORACLE. YOUR HOLO-ROOM...
SSH. BOTH OF YOU.
THERE'S SOMETHING VERY STRANGE GOING ON.
LIKE A MASSIVE ENERGY DRAIN...
UH... GUYS? GUYS?

HELLO, LADIES.
ALLOW ME TO INTRODUCE MYSELF...
WHAT THE...
GREAT. IT'S...
SHADOW THIEF.

I SEE MY REPUTATION PRECEDES ME. AS DOES...
...DEATH!

HE'S MINE.
FINE BY ME.
BATGIRL, WAIT-- HE'S INTANGIBLE. HE'S USING A THANAGARIAN--
--SHADOW FIELD.
I KNOW.
SILLY GIRL.
HOW WILL YOU FIGHT SOMETHING YOU CAN'T HIT?
YOU TELL ME.

NICE SWORD.
WANT IT?
YOU LITTLE...
SHOULDN'T WE...? SHOULD I...?
STAY PUT. SHE KNOWS WHAT SHE'S DOING.
SOMEHOW...

LET'S GO...
..."NINJA".

NICE.

SECRET KOGA-RYU TECHNIQUES!
WHO TAUGHT YOU THOSE?!
YOU DID. JUST NOW.

I'M SETTING EVERYTHING TO POWER DOWN SO IT WON'T SHORT, AND THEN MY GENERATOR'S GOING TO SWITCH POLARITY ON THE CURRENT, WHICH SHOULD DISABLE HIS--
--OH, JUST LIGHT THE DAMN CANDLE.
WHY AM I LIGHTING A CANDLE? WE'RE NOT GOING TO HOLD A PRAYER VIGIL OR SOMETHING, ARE WE?
SHADOW THIEF'S NOT SUPER-HUMAN. HE'S WEARING AN ALIEN DEVICE THAT'S DRAWING POWER FROM MY SYSTEM.
THERE.

NOW YOU CAN GO HELP.
HELP ME.
UH... THREE BREATHS...
I KNOW. START COMPRESSIONS.

GASP...
PULSE IS GOOD. HE'S OKAY.
HE'S GOING TO BE OKAY.
DIDN'T... MEAN...
PLEASE... I...
ORACLE...
HEY.
ALL I SEE HERE IS AN UNCONSCIOUS VILLAIN.
THANKS. I'LL...
...BE BACK.

ONE YEAR FROM NOW, WE FIGHT.
YOU MUST USE ALL YOUR SKILLS. YOUR *KILLING* SKILLS.
AND I'LL USE MINE.
A DEATH-DUEL. AS BEFITS WARRIORS.
WHAT IS YOUR ANSWER?
YES.

VIDEO LOGS
RIDDLER
ROYAL FLUSH GANG
SANDRA KAY
SCARECROW
SCIROCCO
SCORCH
SHADOW THIEF
SHIVA
SHRAPNEL
SILVER BANSHEE
SINESTRO
SOLOMON GRUNDY
STARBREAKER
STARRO
SUDDEN DEATH
TALIA
TEMPTRESS
TERRA-MAN
TOYMAN
LADY SHIVA
FILE
SUPER-VILLAIN FILE
ACCESSED 304 TIMES
AUTO REPLAY
KELLEY PUCKETT Writer
DAMION SCOTT Penciller
ROBERT CAMPANELLA Inker
JOHN COSTANZA Letterer
GREGORY WRIGHT Colorist
DIGITAL CHAMELEON Separator
MICHAEL WRIGHT Editor
THE END

SURE SHE'S OKAY?
SHE'S FINE.
YOU SURE? I'VE BEEN HERE TWO HOURS AND SHE HASN'T MOVED ONCE.
SURE SHE'S NOT IN A COMA OR ANYTHING?

I'M *SURE*. SHE'LL WAKE UP AND EAT SOMETHING EVENTUALLY. SHE JUST NEEDS A LOT OF REST.
REALLY? HOW MUCH IS A LOT?
WELL, SHE'S BEEN SLEEPING ABOUT TWENTY HOURS A DAY.
WHOA. THAT'S A LOT.
AND SHE'S BEEN DOING THIS FOR THREE DAYS?
UH... ACTUALLY, IT'S NOW BEEN FOUR.

JEEZ... AREN'T YOU WORRIED AT ALL?
HEY, SHE'S BATGIRL.
LOOK, YOU KNOW WHAT SHE'S LIKE. SHE CAN COME BACK FROM ANYTHING.
BESIDES, SHE JUST BECAME THE FIRST PERSON IN HISTORY TO BEAT SHIVA SINGLE-HANDEDLY.
HER INJURIES AREN'T REALLY THAT SERIOUS, ALL THINGS CONSIDERED.
IT JUST... WELL, THE FIGHT TOOK A LOT OUT OF HER, PHYSICALLY, MENTALLY AND, UH, SPIRITUALLY.
SO... WHAT HAPPENED, EXACTLY?
I'M NOT SURE. THEY FOUGHT AT SOME TEMPLE DEVOTED TO THE WORSHIP OF SHIVA, AND BATGIRL WON.
OH, BUT FIRST SHIVA KILLED HER AND THEN BROUGHT HER BACK TO LIFE.
WHAT?

YEAH, THAT GOT MY ATTENTION, TOO. UNFORTUNATELY, I HAVEN'T REALLY GOTTEN MUCH MORE OUT OF--
OH...NO.
WHAT'S UP?
SOMETHING NOT GOOD.
...TAKE YOU TO GAZETTE SQUARE, WHERE A MAN HAS TAKEN A WOMAN HOSTAGE.
WE'RE NOT SURE WHAT HIS DEMANDS ARE AT THIS POINT...
NAILS
SOMETHING NOT GOOD AT ALL.
...BUT HE'S BEEN RANTING ABOUT "THE DESTROYER OF THE DESTROYER OF WORLDS..."
"I AM BECOME DEATH, THE DESTROYER OF WORLDS."
IT'S FROM THE BHAGAVAD-GITA.
HE'S TALKING ABOUT THE ONE WHO TOOK SHIVA DOWN.

HE'S CALLING BATGIRL OUT.
OOH.
YEAH.
ALL RIGHT. WELL. GUESS I'M OFF.
WHAT? NO. YOU CAN'T. THIS GUY--
--LOOKS LIKE HE BELONGS TO THAT CULT THAT WORSHIPS SHIVA. IF HE DOES AND BATGIRL DOESN'T SHOW...
...WHO KNOWS WHAT THE REST OF THE CULT WILL DO.
EXACTLY. YOU COULD CALL IN NIGHTWING OR ROBIN, BUT THAT'D TAKE TOO LONG AND MIGHT JUST GET THE REST OF THE CULT GOING.
NOPE. IT NEEDS TO BE A FEMALE. IT'S GONNA HAVE TO BE ME.
DON'T BE SO WORRIED. I'VE GONE UP AGAINST TOUGH GUYS BEFORE.
THIS IS WHAT BATMAN TRAINED ME TO DO. PIECE O' CAKE.

DON'T FORGET TO--
UH-HUH.
REMEMBER THAT--
RIGHT.
WATCH OUT FOR--
GOT IT.
AND MAKE SURE YOU--
OKAY ALREADY!
SHEESH.

YOU'D THINK I'D NEVER GONE UP AGAINST A PSYCHOTIC HOSTAGE-HOLDING MARTIAL ARTS MASTER WHO WANTS TO KILL BATGIRL BEFORE.
I CAN DO THIS.
I CAN TOTALLY DO THIS.
I CAN'T DO THIS.

SURE YOU CAN.
YEAH, RIGHT. LOOK, I'M NOT LIKE YOU-- IN FACT, NO ONE IS--
YOU JUST KINDA APPEAR IN GOTHAM ALL OF A SUDDEN, NO ONE KNOWS WHERE YOU CAME FROM, AND BOOM--
--YOU'RE THE NEW BATGIRL.
YOU'VE GOT THESE INSANE ABILITIES AND I'M NOT EVEN SURE YOU'RE NOT A METAHUMAN, AND YOU BARELY EVEN LOOK AT ME, MUCH LESS TALK...
AND NOW THIS GUY HAS A HOSTAGE AND HE'S IN A PUBLIC PLACE AND HE WANTS TO KILL ME...
...WELL, *YOU*... AND EVERYTHING'S STACKED ON HIS SIDE.
AND I TOTALLY THOUGHT I COULD TOTALLY HANDLE THIS AND NOW I'M THINKING THAT I CAN'T.
SO IF SOMETHING'S NOT WORKING, CHANGE IT. TAKE CONTROL.
MAKE IT WORK FOR YOU.
BATMAN TRUSTS YOU. ORACLE TRUSTS YOU. *YOU* JUST NEED TO TRUST YOU.
YOU CAN DO THIS.

ALL RIGHT! LOOKIN' GOOD.
NOW I JUST HAVE TO MAKE SURE HE'S FOLLOWING...
...AND...
PERFECT.
WASN'T EXPECTING HIM TO BE QUITE THIS QUICK, THOUGH...
NO PROBLEM. LEAD HIM SOMEPLACE OUT OF THE WAY. JUST MAKE SURE I DON'T MAKE ANY--
--MISTAKES--

BROOSH!
OW.

CRASH!
OW!

RROK!
OW!

OF COURSE.

HOW APPROPRIATE.
PLEASE.

WHAT *IS* THIS PLACE?
THE SCENE OF YOUR GREATEST TRIUMPH, OF COURSE.

IT IS WHERE I SHALL REGAIN MY HONOR.
WHEN SHIVA ENTERED THE TEMPLE, I FLED WITH THE OTHERS. I DID NOT STAND BY MY MASTER'S SIDE AS I HAD FOR SO MANY YEARS.
I TOO SHOULD HAVE WELCOMED THE GLORIOUS DEATH SHIVA WOULD BRING, AS MY MASTER DID.

WHEN I RETURNED LATER THAT NIGHT, I SAW THAT THE IMPOSSIBLE HAD OCCURRED. SHIVA HAD BEEN DEFEATED.
AND SO WAS I GRANTED A CHANCE TO RESTORE MY HONOR. BY DYING A VALIANT DEATH AT THE HANDS OF THE ONE WHO DEFEATED SHIVA.
MY LIFE IS YOURS. TAKE IT.
KILL ME.
YEAH... LISTEN, I'M NOT GOING TO--
THE RITUALS MUST BE OBSERVED. I WOULD NOT WISH TO INSULT YOU BY IMPLYING OTHERWISE.
THIS, THEN, SHALL BE A FIGHT TO THE DEATH, NO MATTER HOW ABSURD THE NOTION THAT I MIGHT POSSIBLY WIN.
OF COURSE.
LET IT BEGIN.

TFF
BAM!
I... I HIT YOU.
I HIT YOU.
THAT'S NOT POSSIBLE.

YOU COULD NOT HAVE DEFEATED THE DESTROYER.
YOU ARE AN IMPOSTOR.
YOU DEFILE THIS TEMPLE!
OH, THAT MAKES SENSE.
I'M NOT A SERIAL KILLER, SO I'M RUINING THE NEIGHBORHOOD.
AH... DO YOU HEAR THAT?
SIRENS. THE POLICE ARE ON THEIR WAY.
KRAK!

EXCELLENT. AFTER I'M DONE WITH YOU, I SHALL SLAY SOME OF GOTHAM'S FINEST.
NICE JOB. YOU REALLY SHOWED HIM.
GUESS I WAS WRONG AFTER ALL. YOU COULDN'T DO IT.
STRONGER... THAN I EXPECTED...
SMARTER TOO. YOU, ON THE OTHER HAND, ARE NOTHING LIKE BATMAN THOUGHT.
I CAN'T BELIEVE HE HAD FAITH IN YOU.
YOU FAILED HIM. YOU FAILED US ALL. AND NOW YOU'RE GOING TO DIE BECAUSE OF IT. WHAT'S WORSE, SO ARE SOME COPS.

SHUT UP!
EXIT

BAM!
WORSHIP THAT.

SCOTT PETERSON
Writer
VINCENT GIARRANO
Penciller
JESSE DELPERDANG
Inker
JASON WRIGHT
Colorist
DIGITAL CHAMELEON
Separator
JOHN COSTANZA
Letterer
MICHAEL WRIGHT
Editor

SO.

FREEZE VISION and JILL
7 GOTHAM news
YUM!
7 GOTHAM news

TAG.
SKRASH
YOU WIN.
HEH, HEH.
YOU KNOW, EVER SINCE YOU BEAT SHIVA...YOU'VE TURNED INTO A REAL--

SH.

COOL. THOSE GUYS LOOK SERIOUS.
YEAH.

THNK

THOK
WHUK
BU-DU-DU-DU-
KROK
THAK
BU-DU-DU-

DOKK

NSA

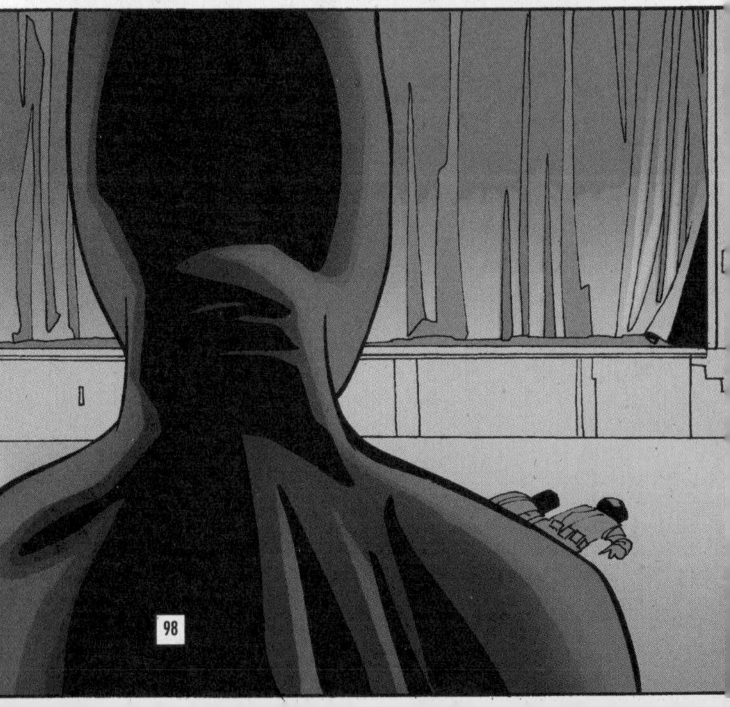

EXIT

CONGRATULATIONS.

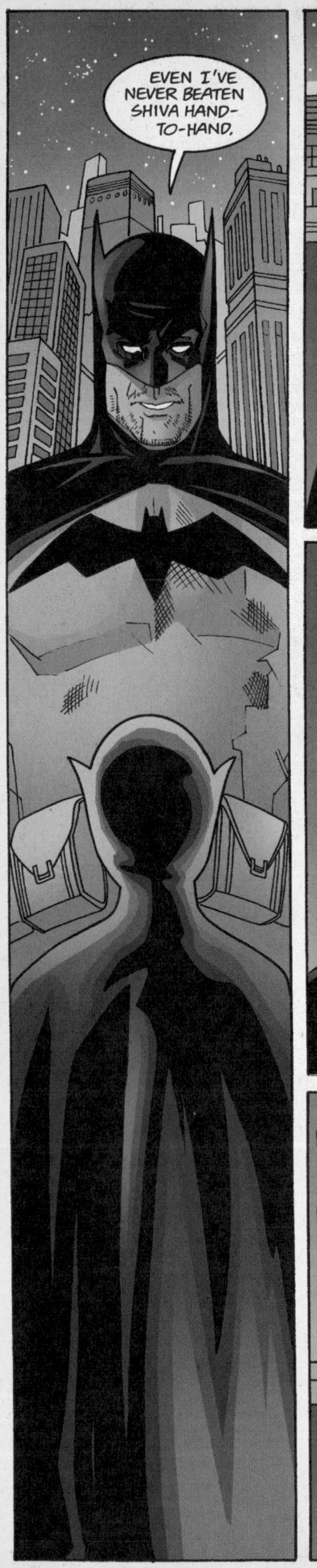
EVEN I'VE NEVER BEATEN SHIVA HAND-TO-HAND.

YOU LOOK... DIFFERENT.

IF YOU SEE MORE OF THOSE TEAMS, STEER CLEAR. THERE'S MORE TO THEM THAN MEETS THE EYE.

WAIT.

I...
ALLEGED MURDERER BRUCE WAYNE STILL AT LARGE
Gotham NEWS
LET ME HELP.
I LET YOU FACE SHIVA, DESPITE THE DANGER, BECAUSE IT WAS SOMETHING YOU HAD TO DO YOURSELF.
YES. THANK YOU.
DON'T THANK ME.
RETURN THE FAVOR.

SHE BROKE MY JAW!
NO.

YES.
NO.
YES.

NO. IF YOUR JAW WERE BROKEN, YOU WOULDN'T BE ABLE TO TALK.
AND MY LIFE WOULD BE MUCH EASIER.

NOW, GO AWAY.
I'M BUSY.
VESPER FAIRCHILD

YOU BROKE HER JAW?
NERVE STRIKE. MAKES A TINY...

...FRACTURE?
RIGHT. TINY.

WELL, HIT HER HARDER NEXT TIME.
NOW, GO AWAY... I REALLY AM BUSY.

I SAW BATMAN.

WHAT'D HE SAY?
NOT MUCH.
"GO AWAY."
OF COURSE. DUMB QUESTION.
SO... ANY CLUES?
"CLUES"? SURE.
DOZENS OF CLUES. HUNDREDS OF CLUES. ROBIN, NIGHTWING AND I'VE BEEN AT IT 'ROUND THE CLOCK FOR THREE WEEKS JUST FOLLOWING ALL THE CLUES.
AND?

AND THEY ALL POINT RIGHT TO BRUCE WAYNE MURDERING VESPER FAIRCHILD.
IF THIS IS A SETUP, IT'S UNLIKE ANYTHING I'VE EVER SEEN.
"IF"?
WHAT "IF"?
RELAX. IT'S... A SLIP OF THE TONGUE...
NO. YOU THINK...?
LOOK AT ME.
LOOK AT ME.
YOU THINK... HE DID IT?!
YOU DO. YOU THINK--
WHAT AM I SUPPOSED TO THINK?!

I DON'T THINK HE DID IT. I'M JUST... FOLLOWING THE EVIDENCE.
LIKE HE TAUGHT US TO.

I'M SORRY.
CAN I... DO SOMETHING?

TELL ME HE DIDN'T DO IT. AND MAKE ME BELIEVE YOU.

THAT'S IT.
REST IN PEACE
VESPER
KATHERINE
FAIRCHILD
OCTOBER 14, 1973-
JANUARY 4, 2002
THANKS.

NOW, GO.
WHY? WHAT'RE YOU--?

WHOA. WAIT A SECOND. YOU'RE NOT THINKING WHAT I THINK YOU'RE THINKING, ARE YOU?

YOU ARE. WHY? THEY ALREADY DID THE AUTOPSY... WHY'S EVERYONE SO FREAKED-OUT ABOUT THIS BRUCE WAYNE CASE?
GO.

NO. THIS... I KNOW YOU'RE ALL DARK AND FREAKY AND STUFF, BUT THIS IS TOO WEIRD.
YOU WANT TO DIG HER UP, YOU'RE GOING TO HAVE TO KNOCK ME OUT AGAIN.

THNK

THUD

I CAN'T BELIEVE YOU DID THAT AGAIN.

I SWEAR I'M GOING TO K-

--OH, GEEZ.

WAYNE'S FIST...
I KNOW... ITS SHAPE.
IF... BRUISES... DIDN'T MATCH...
BUT I,.. CAN'T TELL, SHE'S TOO...
...DECOMPOSED.
YOU'RE RIGHT.
THIS... WAS WRONG.
SORRY... MISS FAIRCHILD.

WAIT.

I HOPE YOU'RE GOING TO WASH THAT HAND...

EW! WHAT ARE YOU DOING?

NERVE STRIKE.

NERVE STRIKE. THAT MAKES NO SENSE AT ALL.

NO, IT DOES NOT. IF YOU'RE BRUCE WAYNE AND YOU KILL VESPER IN A FIT OF RAGE, WHY WOULD YOU EVER USE A NERVE STRIKE?

BUT IF YOU'RE SETTING BRUCE WAYNE UP, AND YOU NEED TO GET VESPER TO WAYNE MANOR WITHOUT CHEMICALS, OR BLUNT TRAUMA, OR SIGNS OF RESTRAINT...

...YOU HIT HER WITH A NERVE STRIKE.
IF YOU KNOW HOW.

THIS IS GOOD.
THIS IS VERY GOOD.

NICE JOB, ELVIRA.

HEY, HOW ABOUT A REMATCH ON THE ROOFTOP TAG?
DOUBLE OR NOTHING.

OH, BUT... I HAVE...
...NO MONEY...

OH, WAIT... THAT'S RIGHT.
YOU... ALWAYS *LOSE*.

YOU'RE IT.

I SWEAR TO GOD, NEXT TIME...
...I'M ROOTING FOR SHIVA.

HELLO? YOU OKAY?
YOU LOOK LIKE YOU COULD USE A REFILL.

KELLEY PUCKETT
Writer
PHIL NOTO
Penciller
ROBERT CAMPANELLA
Inker
JASON WRIGHT
Colorist
DIGITAL CHAMELEON
Separator
JOHN COSTANZA
Letterer
MICHAEL WRIGHT
Editor

RING RING
RING RING
RING RING
RING RING

BATGIRL.

SPOILER.
HEY. AM I... INTERRUPTING?
OH. YEAH. TRAINING. ABOUT THAT...
BATMAN WAS TRAINING ME, BUT HE'S... GONE OR SOMETHING. SO I WAS WONDERING IF... MAYBE YOU COULD SHOW ME... SOME OF YOUR MOVES.
NO. TOO BUSY.
WITH WHAT?

MY TRAINING.
OH, COME ON... YOU CAN TAKE A COUPLE DAYS OFF.
I MEAN... YOU ALREADY BEAT LADY SHIVA. WHO ARE YOU TRAINING FOR, SUPERMAN?
PRETTY PLEASE? I'LL BE YOUR BEST FRIEND.
YOU... WON'T LAST.
TRY ME.

BLEEUGH
KOFF KOFF
MMF
WOW.
SO...
...SAME TIME TOMORROW?
SURE.

RING RING
RING RING
SO WHAT DOES SHE KNOW?

NOTHING. YOUR TEAM WAS A RANDOM ENCOUNTER.
SO WHY ARE YOU STILL THERE?
I'M EVALUATING HER.
"EVAL--"? YOU CAN'T BE SERIOUS.
WITH HER... AFFILIATION? THINK OF THE RISKS. HOW COULD SHE POSSIBLY BE WORTH IT?
SHE TOOK YOUR MEN OUT IN UNDER THREE SECONDS. WORTH A LOOK, DON'T YOU THINK?
SHE GOT LUCKY. IT'D BE DIFFERENT IF THEY WERE EXPECTING HER.
THINK SO? LET'S FIND OUT.

HEY.
HEY...
...WHAT'S WRONG?
NOTHING, LET'S GET STARTED.

I...
YOU WOULDN'T UNDERSTAND.
WHAT?

YOU PROBABLY DON'T KNOW... MY FATHER WAS A SUPER-VILLAIN. "THE CLUEMASTER."
LIKE THE RIDDLER, BUT WITH DUMBER HINTS.
HE'S THE REASON I STARTED DOING ALL THIS. TO STOP HIM. HE USED TO...
WELL, ANYWAY. NOT IMPORTANT NOW.
I WAS ON MY WAY OVER HERE WHEN I SAW A SIGN FOR FATHER'S DAY, AND I JUST... I DON'T KNOW. IT CAME BACK TO ME ALL AT ONCE.
YOU CAN'T IMAGINE WHAT IT'S LIKE... TO LIVE WITH SOMEONE LIKE THAT. TO LOOK UP TO HIM AND THEN FIND OUT...
ANYWAY.
SORRY.
HEY...

...NOBODY EVER TALKS ABOUT YOUR PARENTS. WHAT WAS YOUR DAD LIKE?
ASSASSIN.
DAVID CAIN.
ARE YOU SERIOUS?
YEAH.
HA HA HA HA
WHAT?

YOU'VE BEEN LISTENING TO ME WHINE ABOUT HAVING THE CLUEMASTER FOR A DAD, WHEN YOUR DAD'S LIKE... THE SCARIEST KILLER ON THE PLANET?
YEAH.
WHEN MY DAD WAS MAD AT ME HE'D LOCK ME IN THE CLOSET--WHAT DID YOURS DO?
SHOT ME.
HEHH HEHH HA
OH, MAN.
I CAN'T BEAT YOU AT *ANYTHING*.

I JUST SENT HER YOUR WAY. I HOPE YOUR MEN HAVE A GOOD CLEANUP CREW WAITING.

WON'T BE NECESSARY. I DIDN'T SEND "MEN."
WHAT?
FORCE 14.

STOP.
YOU WERE SWINGING. YOUR LINE SLIPPED AND YOU LANDED HARD, INJURING YOUR RIBS.
GO HOME NOW.
IDIOT.

ARE YOU OKAY? WHAT HAPPENED?
IT'S... DUMB.
JUST WATCH... THE RIBS... OKAY?
WELL, ACTUALLY I CAME TO TELL YOU... I WON'T BE WASTING YOUR TIME ANYMORE.
WHAT?
YEAH, SOME... STUFF'S COME UP WITH... TIM. AND OTHER STUFF. ANYWAY, I WON'T BE AROUND AS MUCH, AND I JUST WANTED TO SAY THANKS.

OH. SURE.
SO. SEE YA.
WE NOW RETURN YOU TO YOUR REGULARLY SCHEDULED SECRET FREAKY NINJA TRAINING.
YEAH. RIGHT.
BYE.
KELLEY PUCKETT
Writer
DAMION SCOTT
Penciller
ROBERT CAMPANELLA
Inker
JOHN COSTANZA
Letterer
JASON WRIGHT
Colorist
DIGITAL CHAMELEON
Separator
MICHAEL WRIGHT
Editor

Covers

LOWE